I Write What is Right!

26 A-Z Daily Affirmations for Children

This book belongs to:

Proverbs 22:6
Train up a child in the way he
should go, and when he is old he
will not depart from it.

Aa

Numbers 13:30
Then Caleb quieted the people before Moses, and said, "Let us go up at once and take possession, for we are well able to overcome it."

able

I am well able.

Bb

1 Corinthians 16:13
Watch, stand fast in the faith,
be brave, be strong.

brave

I am brave.

Cc

Romans 8:37
Yet in all these things we are more than conquerors through Him who loved us.

conqueror

I am more than a conqueror

Dd

Proverbs 12:24
The hand of the diligent will rule, But the lazy man will be put to forced labor.

diligent

I am diligent.

Ee

Colossians 3:12
Therefore, as the elect of God, holy and beloved, put on tender mercies, kindness, humility, meekness, longsuffering;

elect

I am the elect of God.

Ff

Ephesians 4:32
And be kind to one another,
tenderhearted, forgiving
one another, even as God in
Christ forgave you.

forgiven

I am forgiven.

Gg

John 1:16
And of His fullness we have all received, and grace for grace.

grace

I have grace.

Hh

Psalm 31:24
Be of good courage,
And He shall strengthen your heart,
All you who hope in the Lord.

hope

I have hope.

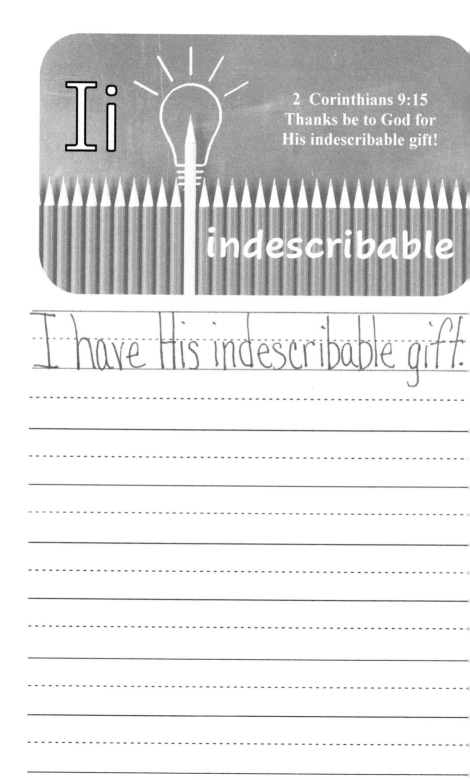

I i

2 Corinthians 9:15
Thanks be to God for
His indescribable gift!

indescribable

I have His indescribable gift.

Jj

John 15:11
"These things I have spoken to you, that My joy may remain in you, and that your joy may be full."

joy

E have joy.

Kk

Romans 12:10
Be kindly affectionate to one another with brotherly love, in honor giving preference to one another;

kind

I am kind.

Ll

1 John 4:7
Beloved, let us love one another, for love is of God; and everyone who loves is born of God and knows God.

love

I show love.

Mm

1 Corinthians 2:16
For "who has known the mind of the Lord that he may instruct Him?" But we have the mind of Christ.

mind

I have the mind of Christ.

Nn

2 Corinthians 5:17
Therefore, if anyone is in Christ,
he is a new creation; old things
have passed away; behold, all
things have become new.

new

I am new in Christ.

Oo

Deuteronomy 28:1
Now it shall come to pass, if you diligently obey the voice of the Lord your God, to observe carefully all His commandments which I command you today, that the Lord your God will set you high above all nations of the earth

obey

I obey the voice of the Lord.

Pp

John 14:27
Peace I leave with you, My peace I give to you; not as the world gives do I give to you. Let not your heart be troubled, neither let it be afraid.

peace

I have Jesus' peace.

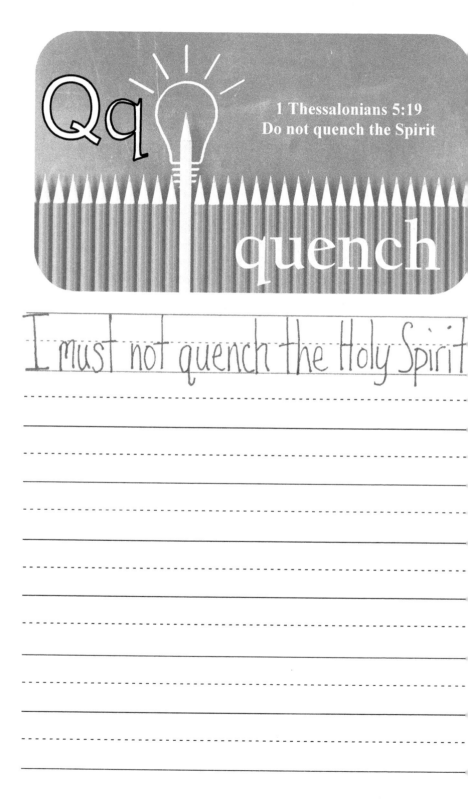

Qq

1 Thessalonians 5:19
Do not quench the Spirit

quench

I must not quench the Holy Spirit

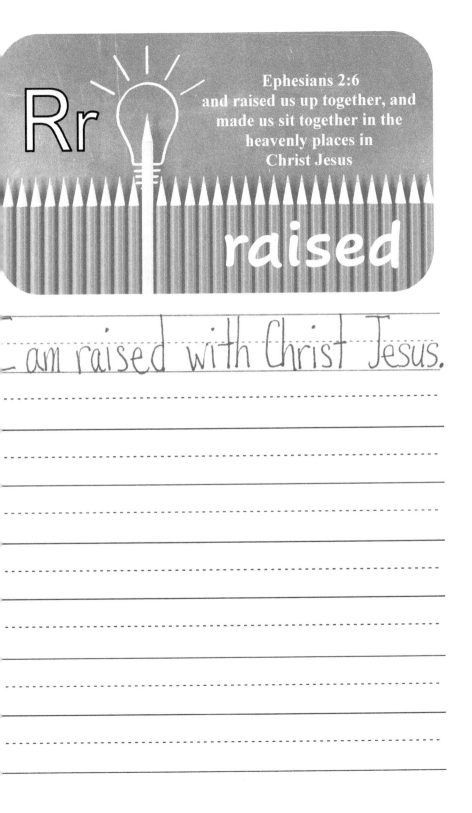

Rr

Ephesians 2:6
and raised us up together, and
made us sit together in the
heavenly places in
Christ Jesus

raised

I am raised with Christ Jesus.

Ss

James 4:7
Therefore submit to God.
Resist the devil and
he will flee from you.

submit

I submit to God.

Tt

John 14:26
But the Helper, the Holy Spirit, whom the Father will send in My name, He will teach you all things, and bring to your remembrance all things that I said to you.

taught

I am taught by the Holy Spirit.

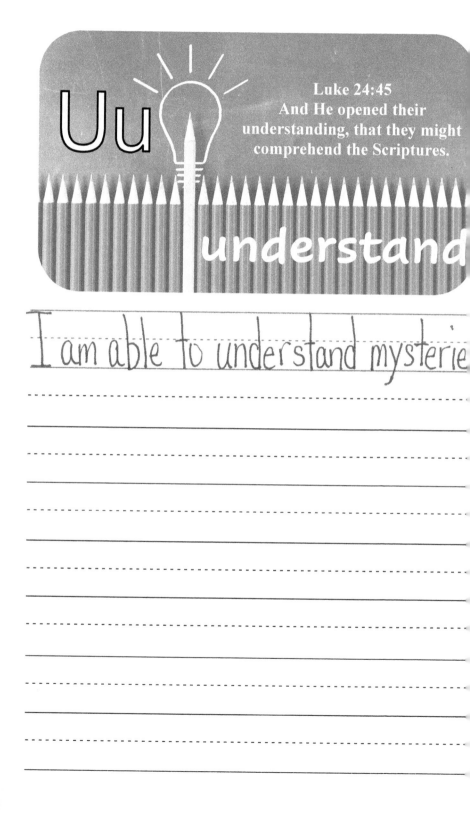

Uu

understand

Luke 24:45
And He opened their understanding, that they might comprehend the Scriptures.

I am able to understand mysterie

Vv

1 Corinthians 15:57
But thanks be to God,
who gives us the victory
through our Lord Jesus Christ

victorious

I am victorious.

Psalm 71:7
I have become as a wonder
to many, But You are
my strong refuge.

Ww

wonder

I am a wonder.

Xx

Psalm 46:10
Be still, and know that I am God;
I will be exalted among the
nations, I will be exalted
in the earth!

e**x**alt

I exalt the Lord.

Yy

Isaiah 26:4
Trust in the Lord forever,
For in Yah, the Lord, is
everlasting strength.

Yah

Yah is my strength.

Zz

Proverbs 23:17
Do not let your heart envy sinners,
But be zealous for the fear of the
Lord all the day;

zealous

I am zealous for the Lord.

Who is Jesus?

Jesus is the Son of God.
He was sent to the earth to
pay the ransom for our sin.
What was broken, is now fixed.

Jesus teaches how to build
the kingdom of heaven, by
activating the kingdom of God,
inside each of us. He also teaches
us to anticipate the glory of
heaven, which is every
believer's eternal home.

Because of Jesus' great love for
us, He paid our sin debt in full
with His precious blood on the
cross. All of us who believe and
accept His gift, enter into right
standing with God and
are heirs of His Kingdom.

You are LOVED.
You were created for great
purpose. You are forgiven of all
wrongdoing. Ask God for help and
guidance each day. Know the Holy
Spirit lives in you and will
comfort, teach, heal,
and empower you.

In Jesus Name,
Amen

Mission: To Proclaim Transformation and Truth

Publisher:	Transformed Publishing, Cocoa, FL
Website:	www.transformedpublishing.com
Email:	transformedpublishing@gmail.com

ISBN: 978-1-953241-28-3

Please Shop

Transformed

Publishing Online:

SCAN ME

(free shipping in the USA for orders of $30 or more)

www.transformedpublishing.com/book-store

CPSIA information can be obtained
at www.ICGtesting.com
Printed in the USA
LVHW081056260122
709349LV00014B/935